Scripture taken from the Holy Bible, NEW INTERNATIONAL VERSION®. Copyright © 1973, 1978, 1984, 2011 by Biblica, Inc. All rights reserved worldwide. Used by permission. NEW INTERNATIONAL VERSION® and NIV® are registered trademarks of Biblica, Inc. Use of either trademark for the offering of goods or services requires the prior written consent of Biblica US, Inc.

WestBow Press books may be ordered through booksellers or by contacting:

WestBow Press
A Division of Thomas Nelson & Zondervan
1663 Liberty Drive
Bloomington, IN 47403
www.westbowpress.com
1 (866) 928-1240

Because of the dynamic nature of the Internet, any web addresses or links contained in this book may have changed since publication and may no longer be valid. The views expressed in this work are solely those of the author and do not necessarily reflect the views of the publisher, and the publisher hereby disclaims any responsibility for them.

Any people depicted in stock imagery provided by Thinkstock are models, and such images are being used for illustrative purposes only.
Certain stock imagery © Thinkstock.

ISBN: 978-1-5127-3008-1 (sc)
ISBN: 978-1-5127-3009-8 (e)

Library of Congress Control Number: 2016902717

Print information available on the last page.

WestBow Press rev. date: 03/11/2016

WestBow
PRESS®
A DIVISION OF THOMAS NELSON
& ZONDERVAN

Lovingly written for Addison, Ainsley, Avery, and our newest one on the way – remember to search for Jesus every day and you will find Him.

With grateful hearts to our parents – Tom and Ruby Stout and Bill and Aline Zell – who taught us early to love Jesus with all our hearts.

LET'S GET STARTED!

Christmas is the most exciting time of year and we hope to make it even more special as you prepare your hearts to welcome Jesus on Christmas morning. Your Stable ADVENTure activity includes a stable play tent, this book of daily devotionals, the Big Star, and a matching picture card game. Each day your children will be searching for the Big Star to find what new item they will look for on their Stable ADVENTure play tent. Every day your children will be learning something special about the birth of Baby Jesus by discovering a new piece of the story and listening to a devotional written especially for that day.

The children's big ADVENTure begins December 1st. To prepare your children for this exciting ADVENTure, show them the Big Star so they will recognize what they will be searching for each morning. The night before (Nov. 30th) or early morning (Dec. 1st) before your children wake up, place the appropriate picture card in the Big Star's back pocket and then hide the Big Star somewhere in your home.

On December 1st, have your children search for the Big Star. On the back of the Big Star is a pocket where you will have placed a picture card for the special item of the day. On the first morning, they will find the Big Star and the "stable" picture card tucked inside the pocket. You and your children will then set up the stable together in preparation for the coming King – Jesus. As you put up the stable, talk about why Jesus is coming (*because He loves us and knows we need a Savior*) and tell your children how much He loves us all. Each day of the Stable ADVENTure we are preparing the stable to welcome Baby Jesus and also preparing our hearts to receive him as Lord and King.

Each morning during the Advent season, your children will wake up to a new search for the Big Star and find a new picture card hidden in the pocket of the Big Star that matches an item on the stable play tent. As they search, remind them how much Jesus wants each of us to search for him every day.

When the Big Star is discovered and the special picture card is revealed, place the Big Star on the front of the stable to shine brightly all day long. Have your children find the matching picture on the stable play tent. Then take time to read the daily devotional book. These short devotionals go along with the picture cards your children will find on their daily searches. The devotionals are intended to add meaning to the items they find and to help the story of Jesus' first advent come alive in your home and hearts. This is a season to celebrate, so celebrate each day as you prepare for the coming King!

Each night after your children have gone to bed, you will want to remove the Big Star from the stable and hide it in a new place. Along with the Big Star, you will also hide the next day's picture card in its back pocket for your children to find in the morning.

As you start your search each day, here is a little song you can sing along with your children. (sung to the tune of *Twinkle, Twinkle Little Star*)

> Twinkle, Twinkle star above,
> lead us to the Gift of love.
> Shining bright to give us light,
> guide us to the Babe tonight.
> Twinkle, twinkle star above,
> lead us to the Gift of love.

Here is a list of what your children will find each day as they search for the Big Star. Make sure you put the new picture card in the Big Star's pocket before the search begins. Happy searching!

December 1st – stable

December 2nd – lantern

December 3rd – rock

December 4th – cow

December 5th – sheep

December 6th – manger

December 7th – stars

December 8th – Mary

December 9th – Joseph

December 10th – donkey

December 11th – innkeeper

December 12 – angelic choir

December 13 – shepherd

December 14th – staff

December 15th – gate

December 16th – shepherd boy

December 17th – big star

December 18th – wise men

December 19th – camel

December 20th – gold

December 21st – frankincense

December 22nd – myrrh

December 23rd – angel

December 24th – Mount Calvary

December 25th – Baby Jesus

The **Matching Card Game** is an additional way to reinforce the message of Jesus' first advent. There are 25 different pictures, and you will find two of each for a total of 50 picture cards. Each morning you will take from the deck of cards the correct picture card to place in the pocket of the Big Star before each day's search. Once the search has been completed, put the picture card back into the deck of 50 and use the cards to play a matching card game.

How to play: Turn all 50 cards face down, mix up the order, and place them in five rows of ten. Each child may take a turn, turning over two picture cards with each turn, trying to find picture cards that match. If a match is found, the player collects the two cards that match, and then tries to find another match. If a match is not found, the two cards are turned back over, and the next player takes a turn. Continue until all cards have found their matches. Count the total cards each player has collected. The player with the most cards is the WINNER! As players find matches, ask what they know about the picture and what part it has in the Nativity Story. Use this game to continue the conversation from the day's devotional.

About our **KJ&me logo**: We designed a logo that expresses who we are and Whose we are. The KJ stands for our Savior, **K**ing **J**esus. Did you notice the crown on the **K** and the children hanging out with King Jesus? Jesus loves all the children of the world and He wants them to hang out with him.

Mary and Joseph had walked a long way
    from their Nazareth home to Bethlehem town.
Their journey was long and because it was late
    now needed a place to lie down.

Knocking on doors, they searched for a room
    but those who they asked shook their heads,
'Our inn is all full, you are much too late
    we have no rooms or beds.'

Tired and hungry, it would soon be dark.
    Oh my, what would they do?
For Mary would soon give birth to her child
    and a child needs a place to come to.

But just as our heavenly Father provides
    for each one of us from the start,
He planned for this hour and already prepared
    a stable of hay and an innkeeper's heart.

So Mary and Joseph and their new son to be
    made their way to where animals feed.
Though it wasn't so clean and probably smelled
    it gave shelter and met all their needs.

And there in a stable, no more humble a place,
    God showed us a part of his plan,
That to welcome his Son as the animals did
    we must open our homes to him.

Stable

Luke 2:7c
"...there was no place for them in the inn."

Let's Pray:

Dear Father in heaven, we want to welcome you into our homes today.

Weary from travel and eager to rest
    Mary and Joseph entered the shelter,
Wondering about the birth of the child
    yet grateful that God was their helper.

The sun was now set and the night was quite dark
    so they needed some light in the stable.
Searching around, Joseph found an old lantern
    and hung it up where he was able.

The lantern shone bright and brought life to the room,
    the animals awakened and stared.
For whenever a light is turned on in the darkness
    the darkness must flee from its glare.

And this is the lesson revealed on that night
    when the lantern was hung in that place;
Jesus would come and bring light to our world,
    the light of his glory and grace.

He is the light as he comes to our hearts
    bringing life as he shines inside.
All who trust him will not live in darkness
    but will have the light of life.

And this is the wonderful story of Christmas,
    that into the darkness did shine
The Light of the World in the form of a child,
    bringing light and life to mankind.

Lantern

John 1:9
"The true light that gives light to every man was coming into the world."

Let's Pray

Dearest Lord Jesus, please shine your light into our lives today so we can shine brightly for you. We love you.

Around the town of Bethlehem
    on the hills and about the homes,
Not many trees or flowers are found,
    but plenty of rocks and stones.

And so it seems fitting to search for a rock
    in our Nativity setting today,
But what can a rock, ordinary and plain,
    about Jesus possibly say?

A rock has strength, is solid and firm,
    on this you can be sure.
Though wind and rain and storms may blow
    a rock is very secure.

And that is why, when building a house,
    a foundation of rock is used.
If the rock is secure and very strong
    the house cannot be moved.

Our rock of strength is Jesus Christ,
    a foundation, sure and strong.
He is the rock that we must use
    to build our lives upon.

And if the winds and storms arise,
    if trouble should come to us,
He is the one we lean upon,
    the Rock in which we trust.

Rock

Psalm 95:1
"Come, let us sing for joy to the Lord; let us shout aloud to the Rock of our salvation."

Let's Pray:

Dear Jesus, we love you so much and want you to be our rock. Help us build our lives on you by trusting you and obeying you every day.

Today we discover a cow in our scene.
 Why a cow? I can hear you ask.
Because cows can teach us particular things
 when cows go about their tasks.

I think that the cows at the stable that night,
 when they witnessed the birth of the boy,
Must have known something special was on,
 must have sensed incredible joy.

Perhaps they knew that the one who created
 all animals and creatures like them,
Was now very near in the form of a babe
 bringing peace and goodwill to all men.

I imagine the cows, when they saw these things,
 joined the angels in chorus to sing.
For cows moo loudly if they want to express
 their views on incredible things.

And something incredible happened that night
 when Jesus our savior was born.
God came to this earth, a servant of men,
 even though he is Savior and Lord.

And that is something that all cows know well,
 as they labor to plow the sod,
Be a helper of men and work in God's field,
 be a servant and workman for God.

COW

Psalm 50:10
"...for every animal of the forest is mine, and the cattle on a thousand hills."

Let's Pray:

Dear Jesus, may we know your peace and
goodwill as we learn to serve each other.

The Lord is our shepherd and knows our needs
   the Psalms of the bible declare.
He guides us and leads us to pastures green
   and we are the flock of his care.

We need not worry when following him,
   and this is our primary task;
To hear when he calls and to follow his lead,
   to do whatever he asks.

That is why sheep were found at the stable
   the night that Jesus was born.
They followed the shepherds who led the way
   to rejoice at the birth of our Lord.

But if sheep don't hear their shepherds voice,
   if they wander away on their own,
They miss their shepherd's love and care,
   are outside the fold and alone.

We all like sheep have gone astray
   and have wandered far from home.
But Jesus left heaven and came to earth
   to search for each wandering one.

This is a lesson for each one of us,
   as close to our Shepherd we live.
If we will but listen, we'll hear his voice
   and discover the love that he gives.

Sheep

Psalm 100:3b
"...we are his people, the sheep of his pasture."

Let's Pray:

Dear Jesus, help us to always follow your
leading and rejoice in your loving care.

A manger is something a carpenter makes
　　to place in his barn filled with hay.
The cows and the donkeys use it to feed
　　when they come in at night for a stay.

Undoubtedly rough and much less than clean,
　　because of how animals eat,
But on this special night it provided a place
　　for a new baby boy to sleep.

And that is a most remarkable thought;
　　that a home for cows and a bed of hay
Would be the first place that God would choose
　　for the Holy One to stay.

Just think how he left the glories of heaven,
　　this Creator and Lord of all,
To come to this earth, become a man
　　and be laid in a manger of straw.

For God so loved the world that he sent,
　　in a gentle and humble way,
The wonderful gift of his only Son
　　asleep on a manger of hay.

That Jesus would come to this earth to dwell
　　and choose to leave heaven above;
Is there any more beautiful story to tell
　　than this wonderful story of love?

Manger

Luke 2:12
"You will find a baby wrapped in cloths and lying in a manger."

Let's Pray:

Dear Jesus, thank you for loving each of us so very much. You are amazing and we love you.

Long ago our Father created the stars,
    he determined their number and place.
They tell the story of his great power
    and proclaim his wonderful grace.

On one special night, far clearer than most,
    the stars twinkled bright in the sky,
For the Light of the World was coming to earth
    and by light do stars testify.

What a great celebration must have been seen
    by the shepherds watching their lambs,
As the stars in the heavens brightened with bliss
    announcing God's wonderful plan.

And all of creation shouted for joy
    as starlight swept over the earth.
The darkness of night was driven away
    by the light of the Savior's birth.

Now whenever we gaze at the nighttime sky
    and consider God's marvelous power,
Those very same stars are shining still
    to remind us of that special hour.

And just as light chases darkness away,
    to reveal what is hidden to men,
So the darkness of sin can be driven away
    by the light of Jesus within.

Stars

Psalm 147:4
"He determines
the number of
the stars and
calls them each
by name."

Let's Pray

Dear Jesus, would you live in our hearts today so we can shine for you?

God sent his angel Gabriel
  to Nazareth, in Galilee.
To speak to a maiden whom he loved
  and announce what soon would be.

Greetings Mary! declared the angel,
  no need for you to fear,
For you are highly favored by God,
  there is something you must hear.

The Lord is near and with you Mary,
  on you his favor rests.
To a baby boy you will give birth,
  all peoples will call you blessed.

This child will be called the Son of God,
  be great and greatly known.
The name of Jesus he shall be given,
  and reign on David's throne.

Mary was greatly troubled at this,
  and asked how it could be true.
So the angel gently spoke to her heart;
  'God's Spirit will come over you.'

'Then here I am, a servant of the Lord,
  to his will I humbly nod.
I do not understand such things,
  but nothing is impossible with God.'

Mary

Luke 1:45
"Blessed is she who has believed that the Lord would fulfill his promises to her!"

Let's Pray:

Dear Lord, thank you for favoring us as your children. As we listen to you today, show us your special plan for our lives. We know you can do anything.

The Bible speaks of a special man
  who chose to do what was right.
An angel appeared to him in a dream
  when he was asleep one night.

And what the angel declared to him
  would forever change his life.
'Do not be afraid,' the angel said,
  'to take Mary home as your wife.'

When Joseph awoke, he obeyed God's word
  because he was a righteous man.
He chose to do right, in spite of the cost,
  submissive to God's great plan.

He gave the baby a special name,
  keeping with the angel's command.
This one named Jesus would save from sin,
  Son of God become Son of Man.

So Joseph took Mary to be his wife,
  loving her and their newborn son.
A simple carpenter chosen by God
  to raise Jesus, the promised one.

You too, like Joseph, can hear God speak,
  you too can choose to obey.
And though at times you don't understand,
  by obeying, you choose God's way.

Joseph

Matthew 1:24
"When Joseph woke up, he did what the angel of the Lord had commanded him and took Mary home as his wife."

Let's Pray:

Dear God, help us like Joseph to do the right things. We want to obey you today.

The Bible speaks of a special man
    who chose to do what was right.
An angel appeared to him in a dream
    when he was asleep one night.

And what the angel declared to him
    would forever change his life.
'Do not be afraid,' the angel said,
    'to take Mary home as your wife.'

When Joseph awoke, he obeyed God's word
    because he was a righteous man.
He chose to do right, in spite of the cost,
    submissive to God's great plan.

He gave the baby a special name,
    keeping with the angel's command.
This one named Jesus would save from sin,
    Son of God become Son of Man.

So Joseph took Mary to be his wife,
    loving her and their newborn son.
A simple carpenter chosen by God
    to raise Jesus, the promised one.

You too, like Joseph, can hear God speak,
    you too can choose to obey.
And though at times you don't understand,
    by obeying, you choose God's way.

Joseph

Matthew 1:24
"When Joseph woke up, he did what the angel of the Lord had commanded him and took Mary home as his wife."

Let's Pray:

Dear God, help us like Joseph to do the right things. We want to obey you today.

Donkey

Caesar Augustus had made a decree
    that the whole Roman world be numbered.
Each man must go to the place of his birth
    to record his family's members.

So Joseph and Mary packed some supplies
    and departed their Nazareth home.
They followed the road to the City of David,
    to the town where Joseph was from.

But travel is hard and can be quite long
    when you are expecting a baby,
So Mary and Joseph brought a donkey along
    to help with the loads they must carry.

Hee Haw! Hee Haw! sang the donkey,
    as they made their way down the road.
He felt he was rather important
    to be chosen to carry their load.

When Mary grew tired and needed to rest
    the donkey would offer his back.
Then Mary would ride and onward they'd go
    till they reached the stable at last.

And that is a glimpse of what Jesus will do,
    as with him we travel life's path.
He will carry our burdens and give us rest
    till at home we are safe at last.

Matthew 11:28
"Come to me, all you who are weary and burdened, and I will give you rest."

Let's Pray:

Dear Jesus, as we think about the night you were born, may we join the little donkey in singing to you. Thank you for carrying our burdens.

We find an innkeeper at the stable today
    peering into his animal's stall.
The glow from a light reflects on his face
    revealing the wonder he saw.

He clearly was curious and wanted to see
    the cause and the source of the light.
So I imagine he quietly stepped outside
    to see the happenings that night.

Who were these shepherds and why had they come
    to the back of his inn at night?
And who was this child they came to see,
    for whom the stars shone bright?

Why did they bow on knee and worship
    with a look of unspeakable bliss?
And why did he think he could hear angels singing
    a psalm of great happiness?

The innkeeper offered a room in his stable
    for the weary travelers to rest.
But now he wants to make room in his heart
    for the one the shepherds confessed.

Just like the shepherds bowed low and worshiped
    and just like the angels proclaimed,
Just like the innkeeper opened his heart,
    you too can make room for the king.

Innkeeper

Luke 15:7
"...there will be more rejoicing in heaven over one sinner who repents than over ninety-nine righteous persons who do not need to repent."

Let's Pray:

We love you, Jesus, and want to make
room for you in our hearts as our King.

Did you peek out the stable window today?
  If so, then what did you see?
A choir of angels, a heavenly host.
  Oh my, how majestic they sing!

Listen closely, I think you will hear their song
  as it echoes throughout the land.
Glory to God in the highest they sing,
  peace on earth and goodwill to men.

Oh, what a wonderful sight to behold
  on that night our savior was born.
Thousands of angels singing with joy
  announcing that Jesus had come.

Did you know God still announces his love
  to each one of us every day?
If we will but look out our windows we'll find
  what all of creation shall say.

The pretty blue sky, the puffy white clouds,
  the sun as it brightens our day,
Remind us that God watches over us all,
  guiding and guarding our way.

God delights in bringing joy to our lives,
  he surrounds us in every way.
If we will take time to look, we'll find
  the wonders of every day.

Angelic
Choir

Luke 2:14
"Glory to God
in the highest,
and on earth
peace to men
on whom his
favor rests."

Let's
Pray:

Dear Lord, thank you for the love you show to us each
and every day. As we celebrate you today, help
us to see you through your beautiful creation.

On the hills near Bethlehem town today
   shepherds still tend to their sheep.
They make them lie down in pastures green
   and give them water to drink.

A shepherd loves and cares for his sheep,
   he watches them night and day.
He guards and protects if an enemy comes
   and chases the wolves away.

A good shepherd shelters his flock with care,
   if injured, he soothes their pain.
The sheep always know their shepherd's voice
   and obey if he calls their name.

Did you know that Jesus refers to himself
   as the Shepherd that tends his sheep?
It may sound strange, but we are his flock,
   and the lambs that he loves to lead.

Just like a shepherd, he cares for his sheep,
   and seeks the ones who stray.
He guards and protects us through our lives,
   watching over us night and day.

If we, like sheep, hear our Shepherd's voice,
   listen closely and follow his lead,
With quiet waters and pastures green
   he'll supply our every need.

Shepherd

John 10:14
"I am the good shepherd; I know my sheep and my sheep know me."

Let's Pray:

Thank you, Jesus, for being our Good
Shepherd. May you provide all we need.

Do you know why a shepherd carries a staff?
  Why it's something important to keep?
Well let me explain, first of all, that a staff
  primarily benefits sheep.

A shepherd will use his staff to lead,
  and we know that sheep need to be led.
He guides and directs his flock so they keep
  on a straight and level path.

If one of his sheep should stumble and fall
  or perhaps gets stuck in a crack.
The shepherd will use his staff to lift
  the animal back on track.

If his sheep should ever come under attack,
  if ever they be alarmed,
The shepherd will use his staff to protect,
  and shield his flock from harm.

And when it is time to come into the pen
  a staff the shepherd will find
To count each and every one of his lambs
  so that none are left behind.

God's word is a staff, a guide for all
  to keep on a level path.
It picks us up when we stumble and fall
  and protects us in every attack.

Staff

Psalm 23:4b
"I will fear no evil, for you are with me; your rod and your staff, they comfort me."

Let's Pray:

We love you, Jesus, and thank you for guiding
us and keeping us safe from all harm.

There is a place that shepherds will use
    to protect their flocks through the night.
A place surrounded by rocks and fence,
    a stronghold, secure and tight.

This stronghold is a refuge for sheep,
    a shelter from wind and storm.
A place where shepherds can lie down and rest,
    a home where lambs can be born.

This sheep pen guards from those who would harm
    the flock in the shepherd's care.
It keeps away robbers prowling around
    and guards against wolves and bears.

There is only one way to enter this fold,
    one way to go out or come in.
A gate is the way and a watchman stands by
    to open the gate to the pen.

In a similar way, our stable maintains
    a gate, inviting us in.
It calls us to leave the world outside
    and draw near to the savior of men.

And just as the stable has only one gate,
    we too have only one way.
The Gate is Jesus and we, his sheep,
    must enter this gate to be saved.

Gate

John 10:7
"...I tell you the truth, I am the gate for the sheep."

Let's Pray:

Dear Father, may we enter through the Gate and so be saved.

That first Christmas eve when Jesus was born
dwelt shepherds in the fields nearby.
Quiet and steady, they kept to their task,
keeping watch over flocks by night.

The day was now gone and the night air cool,
the stars shone bright in the sky.
The shepherd boys warmed themselves by a fire,
whispering and gazing on high.

Then an angel from heaven swiftly appeared
and God's glory shone all around.
The shepherds were startled and very afraid,
trembling, they fell to the ground.

'Do not be afraid, I bring you good news;
for to you a savior is born.
This is the sign that is given to you;
in a manger you'll find the Lord.'

Suddenly, there appeared with the angel
a host of the heavenly guests,
They were praising and singing, 'Peace to all
on whom God's favor rests.'

So to shepherd boys the angels first came
to announce the birth of the King.
Just imagine what it must have been like
to hear the angels sing!

Shepherd Boy

Luke 2:20 "The shepherds returned, glorifying and praising God for all the things they had heard and seen..."

Let's Pray:

Dear Jesus, how we love you as our King. May our family hear the great news of your coming.

God's people waited long for a savior,
and waiting is a difficult thing.
Yet they searched the scriptures and understood
that God would someday send a king.

The one to come would rule all nations,
bringing peace to every land.
A king far greater than any other,
and his kingdom would never end.

From reading the scriptures they also learned
the time that the king would come.
A star would appear to brightly announce
his arrival to everyone.

Do you think they looked for the star every night?
I think that I would, would you?
The star meant the birth of the coming king
and a time when all is made new!

Yet as they waited, the years passed by
and the star was yet to be seen.
But God is faithful, at just the right time,
the star would announce the king.

And the star did rise in the sky one night,
proclaiming the king had been born.
The promised one had come to earth
to reign forevermore.

Big Star

Numbers 24:17b
"A star will come out of Jacob; a scepter will rise out of Israel."

Let's Pray:

Dear Jesus, as we search for the star each day, teach us to seek you always.

Long ago there were those who searched the skies
    looking for a particular sign.
For the prophets of old told of a time
    when the stars would herald a king.

So those who were wise looked up to the stars
    and patiently waited to see
If this was the time the stars would align
    to announce the birth of the king.

In the fullness of time, a star did arise
    and shone bright in the sky one night.
The wise men rejoiced, they now understood
    that the time had finally arrived.

They loaded their camels and prepared to go
    over deserts and mountains far,
To worship the One they longed to see,
    being led by this heavenly star.

Their travel was slow, their journey was long,
    yet they eagerly followed the sign.
For it led to a child destined to be
    the savior of all mankind.

The wise men bowed low and worshiped this king
    bringing incense and myrrh and gold.
Their journey complete, God's promise fulfilled!
    A story the heavens foretold.

Wise Men

Matthew 7:24
"...everyone who hears these words of mine and puts them into practice is like a wise man who built his house on the rock."

Let's Pray:

Dear Jesus may we be wise like the wise men and worship you as our King.

What can you find as you search today
    to add to our nativity scene?
Do you think that camels were actually there?
    If so, then what did they bring?

Camels are lanky, and sometimes look funny
    with one hump or sometimes with two.
Their feet are quite large and so is their tummy,
    and they make silly faces at you.

But camels are big and camels are strong
    and can gallop across the land.
They carry great loads when the journey is long
    and can walk through the blowing sand.

So it must have been camels that came that day
    with the wise men who followed the star.
And they must have been loaded with all it took
    to make such a trek from afar.

But it was more than goods these animals bore,
    for they also carried some treasure.
They brought great gifts to the newborn king,
    gold and incense and myrrh.

And just like the camels were thrilled long ago
    to give gifts to the newborn king.
We too have a treasure, and it is this:
    the gift of our hearts to bring.

Camel

Matthew 2:11 "...they opened their treasures and presented him with gifts..."

Let's Pray:

Jesus, may we run to you in love and obedience
and bring to you the gift of our hearts.

The bible tells of a wonderful gift
    the wise men brought from afar.
A special gift for a special child
    and one that is costly and rare.

A gift of gold is a gift of love
    for it speaks of value and worth.
To bring such a gift to a newborn child
    explains his future at his birth.

It shows the purpose God had for his life
    and the reason for which he came.
It proclaims that he is the Lord of all,
    and foretells of his glorious reign.

As a king he will rule over all other kings;
    they will bow before him and say,
That Jesus is Lord over all the earth
    to God's glory and marvelous praise.

His kingdom will be a wonderful place
    when he fixes all that is wrong.
Where the proud are humbled, the least are great,
    and those once weak are strong.

So wise men brought gold to worship the king
    and we too can bring him our best.
If we will confess that Jesus is Lord
    we will enter his kingdom of rest.

Gold

Revelation 19:16 "On his robe and on his thigh he has this name written: KING OF KINGS AND LORD OF LORDS"

Let's Pray:

Jesus, as we worship you today, may
we always give you our best.

Wise men brought with them a second gift
    to give to God's holy son.
A gift foretelling what Jesus would do
    in service for everyone.

The gift was incense and used by priests
    to minister before the Lord.
It was burned with fire and its smoke would rise,
    a sweet smelling offering to God.

The rising smoke is a picture of prayer
    rising up to our Father in heaven.
The sweetness reminds us that God will accept
    our prayers when offered to him.

As priests would plead for the people in prayer,
    so Jesus would plead for us.
Like the incense offered to God above,
    so Jesus would offer himself.

And just as the incense would rise to God,
    accepted, a sweet sacrifice,
So someday Jesus would rise from the dead,
    accepted and pleading for us.

Wise men brought incense for the newborn child
    to teach us that Jesus would be
Our great High Priest in service to God,
    living always to intercede.

Frankincense

Psalm 110:4
"The Lord has sworn and will not change his mind: 'You are a priest forever...'"

Let's Pray.

Dear Lord Jesus, we thank you for caring for us
and telling your Father about us each day.

Long ago, the wise men carried their gifts
     to give to the newborn child.
Each gift taught something about the One
     born humbly, meek and mild.

Gold meant that Jesus would be a king,
     his kingdom forever will be.
Incense spoke of priestly things,
     his prayers for you and me.

But another gift was also borne,
     a cherished jar of myrrh.
A curious gift, a kind of perfume,
     costly, sweet and pure.

But what could perfume do for a child?
     And what would its value be?
The answer lies in who Jesus is,
     and a place called Calvary.

Myrrh was mixed with aloes and spices
     and used when somebody died.
It perfumed the body, wrapped with cloth,
     then hardened as it dried.

So myrrh told the story of what would be
     when this baby grew to a man.
He came to die for the sins of the world,
     be buried and rise again.

Myrrh

Deuteronomy 18:18 "I will raise up for them a prophet like you from among their fellow Israelites…"

Let's Pray:

Thank you, heavenly Father, that Jesus is alive today
and that we too can be alive with him forever!

An angel named Gabriel was sent by God
    to announce that Jesus would come.
He greeted Mary saying she was blessed,
    and would soon give birth to a son.

The angel also appeared to Joseph
    and told him to not be ashamed.
Encouraged he was to make Mary his wife,
    to the child give a special name.

And on that great night when Jesus was born,
    it was angels to shepherds who came.
Good news of great joy the angels proclaimed.
    'Glory to God,' the angels sang.

You see, all angels are servants of God,
    he sends them to minister to men.
Some angels are sent to announce his word,
    some sent to fight battles for him.

They are awesome in strength, mighty in power,
    they stand in the presence of God.
They forever are singing their praises to him,
    to whom all praise belongs.

God commands his angels, the bible says,
    to keep watch over you and me.
It is awesome to think God loves us so much,
    his angels our lives oversee.

Angel

Matthew 18:10
"See that you do not look down on one of these little ones. For I tell you that their angels in heaven always see the face of my Father in heaven."

Let's Pray:

Dear God, thank you for watching over us
and for protecting us with your angels.

Today we look beyond our scene
   of stable hay and manger.
Beyond the view of shepherd boys
   and kings bowed to the savior.

Look closely through the stable window
   and tell me what you see.
Away in the distance, a lonely hill,
   and rugged crosses three.

Our window speaks of a future time
   beyond our savior's birth.
It speaks of God's salvation plan
   and why he came to earth.

For Jesus on that cross someday
   would die for all our sins.
To give his life, a sacrifice,
   that we might live with him.

So as we celebrate this day,
   we see God's amazing plan.
The Son of God would come to earth
   and die as Son of Man.

O wondrous thought, that he would come
   for this and nothing less;
That we be free from all our sins,
   and eternal life possess.

Mt. Calvary

John 3:16
"For God so loved the world that he gave his one and only Son, that whoever believes in him shall not perish but have eternal life."

Let's Pray:

Dearest Lord Jesus, thank you for dying for our sins so we can live with you forever.

On this Christmas day our souls rejoice,
    giving glory to our great Lord.
For he has remembered us in our need
    and fulfilled his promised word.

That word, spoken by prophets of old,
    foretold that a savior would come,
That he would be great, and as God's Son
    for a time would make earth his home.

Now Jesus has come to dwell with us,
    Son of God became Son of Man.
To each of us a child has been given,
    the heart of God's marvelous plan.

He comes to us now, so that we can know
    the joy and peace that he brings,
So that we, along with the angel choir,
    might rise with our voices and sing.

Wonderful Counselor, Mighty God,
    Prince of Peace is he.
From this time on the world is blessed
    and never the same will be.

As our stable welcomes the child this day,
    shepherds and wise men and star,
We too can welcome Jesus this day,
    inviting him into our hearts.

Baby
Jesus

1 John 4:9
"This is how
God showed
his love among
us: He sent
his one and
only Son into
the world that
we might live
through him."

Let's
Pray:

Dearest Lord Jesus, as we celebrate your birthday today may
we invite you into our hearts and welcome you into our lives.